My World

KU-320-501

Time

Ann Peat

Raintree

www.raintreepublishers.co.uk
Visit our website to find out more information about **Raintree** books.

To order:
☎ Phone 44 (0) 1865 888112
🗎 Send a fax to 44 (0) 1865 314091
🖥 Visit the Heinemann Bookshop at **www.raintreepublishers.co.uk** to browse our catalogue and order online.

First published in Great Britain by Raintree, Halley Court, Jordan Hill, Oxford OX2 8EJ, part of Harcourt Education.
Raintree is a registered trademark of Harcourt Education Ltd.

© Harcourt Education Ltd 2003
The moral right of the proprietor has been asserted.

All rights reserved. No part of this publication may be reproduced, stored in a retrieval system, or transmitted in any form or by any means, electronic, mechanical, photocopying, recording, or otherwise, without either the prior written permission of the publishers or a licence permitting restricted copying in the United Kingdom issued by the Copyright Licensing Agency Ltd, 90 Tottenham Court Road, London W1T 4LP (www.cla.co.uk).

Editorial: Charlotte Guillain and Diyan Leake
Design: Michelle Lisseter
Picture Research: Maria Joannou
Production: Lorraine Hicks

Originated by Dot Gradations
Printed and bound in China by South China Printing Company

ISBN 1 844 21271 8
07 06 05 04 03
10 9 8 7 6 5 4 3 2 1

British Library Cataloguing in Publication Data
Peat, Ann
Time
529
A full catalogue record for this book is available from the British Library.

Acknowledgements
The publishers would like to thank the following for permission to reproduce photographs: Action Plus p. **4**; Trevor Clifford p. **5**; Digital Vision p. **19**; Sylvia Cordaiy Photo Library p. **8**; Topham Picturepoint p. **6**; Tudor Photography pp. **7, 9, 10, 11, 12, 13, 14, 15, 16, 17, 18, 20, 21, 22, 23**.

Cover photograph, reproduced with permission of Tudor Photography.

Every effort has been made to contact copyright holders of any material reproduced in this book. Any omissions will be rectified in subsequent printings if notice is given to the publishers.

DUDLEY PUBLIC LIBRARIES
L 4669
654961   SCH
        J 529

Contents

Some words are shown in bold, **like this.** You can find them in the glossary on page 23.

How long does it take to do things?

We can do some things very quickly.

When we run in a race, we try to go as fast as we can.

A train journey might take a whole day or more.

The train goes quickly, but it goes a long way.

What happens in the day time?

People go to work in the day time.

When there is daylight, people can see clearly to do things.

Children go to school in the day time.

There is enough light to do things outdoors.

What happens at night time?

It is dark at night time.

Outside, the moon may be bright in the sky.

We go to sleep at night time.

We need a light to see things at night.

What happened yesterday?

Yesterday these people went to the shop.

They bought things to make
a cake today.

What is happening today?

Today these people are using the things they bought yesterday.

They are making a cake.

What will happen tomorrow?

Tomorrow there will be a birthday party.

It will be time to eat the cake!

What do we do on weekdays?

On weekdays children go to school.

Monday   Tuesday   Wednesday

Most adults do their work on weekdays.

Thursday   Friday

What do we do at the weekend?

There is no school at the weekend.

People can go for a walk to the park.

Saturday

The weekend is a time when families can do things together.

Sunday

What do we use to tell the time?

Clocks and **watches** show us minutes and hours.

Some clocks go up to 12 hours and some go up to 24 hours.

FEBRUARY

MONDAY	TUESDAY	WEDNESDAY	THURSDAY	FRIDAY	SATURDAY	SUNDAY
					1	2
3	4	5	6	7	8	9
10	11	12	13	14	15	16
17	18	19	20	21	22	23
24	25	26	27	28		

A **calendar** shows us days, weeks and months.

Calendars show us all the days in a whole year.

What time is it?

What times do the clocks say?

What do you do at that time?

Glossary

calendar
pages that show the days and months of the year

clock
something we can use to tell the hours in the day

watch
small clock that people can wear, usually on the wrist

Index